# 30 WAYS TO PLEASE YOUR MAN
By DeShai Cole

# 30 WAYS TO PLEASE YOUR MAN
## A guide for in and out of the bedroom

*By DeShai Cole*

Photography by Touché Harvey
www.touchestudios.com

<u>Models</u>
Christopher Bonner

Lira Galore
www.liragalore.com

Bad Girls Club's Mehgan James
twitter.com/mehganjames

<u>Crew</u>
Moni Pradier (Make-Up)
twitter.com/moniP10

Lauren Carmon (Styling/Design)
www.ilovetheboutique.com

# Thank You...

I'd like to dedicate this book to my beautiful daughter Mikiah Bell. Mommy loves you and thanks you for giving me a reason to work my butt off. You won't be reading this until your wedding day!

To my best friend, husband and manager Tim D. of NerdBoyz Entertainment: Thank you for believing in me and my dream, and most of all thanks for supporting me in every way. I love you baby.

To the Byrd, Cole, Davidson, Smith, Thomas and Williams families I love you guys so much thanks for all the support

Thanks to my wonderful circle of friends for your support.

Thanks to the entire DeShai Cole Branding and Grown Woman Talk Entertainment team.

To my Grandmother Mary Jean and Daddy I hope you're proud. I love you and miss you dearly.

Last but not least thank you! Thank you for spending your hard earned money on this book. I hope you love it!

**\*\*\*\*\*\*\*\*\***

# Table of Contents

# Preface

Keeping it spicy in the bedroom can be a task, and coming up with ideas on how to please your man can be stressful as hell! You don't want to find yourself bored when it comes to your sex life. You may be saying "damn, is it really that important to please him?" The answer is; heck yeah! The next question may be "Does he deserve it?" Lets find out! Take the *"To cater or not to cater"* quiz below.

---

### To cater or not to cater

*Directions: Decide if the statement is TRUE or FALSE. If it's true write T in the blank. If it's false write F in the blank.*

_____ 1) My man is hard working and is a great provider.

_____ 2) My man treats me like the Queen I am.

_____ 3) My man does most of the catering in our relationship.

_____ 4) Most of the time my man pays when we go out.

_____ 5) My man rarely buys things for himself.

_____ 6) My man does most of the work during sex.

_____ 7) My man is a great father to our children.

_____ 8) My man always puts me first.

_____ 9) My man isn't afraid to show his love for me.

_____ 10) My man is there for me physically and emotionally.

---

Okay ladies, if you answered TRUE to eight or more, then your man without a doubt deserves to be catered to Boobies!

Now that we've gotten that out of the way, let's move on to the good stuff! I know that there is some fly girl reading this saying "I don't need help pleasing my man honey child!" First let me say "TOOT-TOOT" to all the DIVAS taking damn good care of their men. There is nothing wrong with tooting your own horn honey, but in the words of Beyoncé; "Trust me you need me"!

Just because you take the time to read this book doesn't mean you aren't good in bed or don't know how to please your man. Reading this book means you know that it takes work to keep a relationship spicy! Reading this book may mean you don't have the damn time to come up with "out of the box" ways to drive him wild. That's where I come in and I've done all the legwork for you. All you have to do is sit back, relax and take it all in. Have no fear DIVAS the "Sexpert" is here and I've got you covered when it comes to matters of great sex.

This book is for the Diva who wants to switch it up for her man in bed. It's for the Diva with an open mind who understands that great sex is a big deal in a relationship. Sometimes, we neglect to take care of our Kings because we're so busy building careers, raising children and trying to just keep up. We may even be a little cocky at times and feel like it's the man's job to do the "pleasing," but that's not true pudding pop! It's time to put your vixen panties on and give him a ride he'll never forget.

Now I must tell you that sex isn't meant to save a relationship and you need to lay a good foundation in any relationship. I tell folks all the time that a couple spends more than seventy percent of their time outside of the bedroom, so if sex is all you have, you don't have very much honey! So because sex is less than half the battle, we'll cover some things to apply outside of the bedroom also. Okay, let's get right into it!

# Let Us Count The Ways!

# 1. TAKE CONTROL

I know you've been taught to be submissive, but it's okay to take the wheel sometimes! Here's one time he won't mind you being bossy.

Tell him tonight you're running the show and what you say goes. If he doesn't obey, MAKE HIM PAY! Men love it when women take a little control in the bedroom.

This doesn't mean you have to do all of the work; it's just a way to spice things up a bit.

# 2. TASTE HIM UPSIDE DOWN

Give him the ultimate oral experience. Lay on your back with you head hanging slightly off of the edge of the bed. Tell him to stand over you and place your hands around his masculine legs.

Then have him squat and insert his penis in and out of your mouth while you rub his legs softly.

---

**Helpful Tip:**

Make sure you move your tongue up and down on the back of his penis and adjust your speed gradually.

He'll have flashbacks for days after!

---

# 3. HIRE A PRIVATE DANCER

He's never getting that damn "threesome" but you can give him the next best thing!

Surprise him with an exotic dancer for two. There are a host of private companies that provide sexy dancers right to your doorstep. Let her dance for the two of you while you tease him and give him a preview of what's to come. You may just get girlfriend/wife of the year for this one!

# 4. DIRTY TALK

A vast majority of men wish their women would learn dirty talk. Let your bad girl alter ego come out and whisper something dirty in his ear.

Talking dirty will make your man perform even better and turn him, and his man part, on making the sex even better.

---

### Helpful Tips:

- Remember to keep a sexy tone.
- Don't think too much! I know this can be hard, I mean thinking is what we do, but just let it flow.
- Start out slow and take it all the way to "nasty street"
- Ask questions like "Do you like this pussy" or "Do I feel good to you".
- Whisper in his ear "I want to taste you" right before you give him oral.
- Let him know you're enjoying yourself.

---

## Fun Fact

*The saying "good sex comes naturally" isn't true! Don't get me wrong, you can meet someone and have great sexual chemistry with him or her; but trust me great sex is something you build on. Things that may please one partner may not translate to someone new. You have to be open to trying new things!*

# 5. THE LOVE SQUATS

Take "Doggie Style" to a new level. Position yourself on your knees with you back arched and have you man get behind you as if you are doing the regular doggie style position. Have you man stand then kneel down in a squat position and enter you from behind.

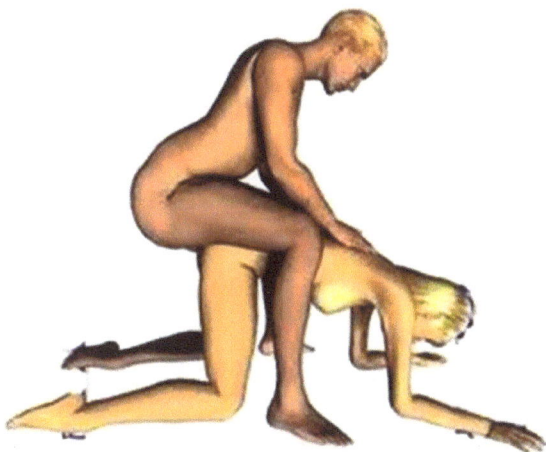

## Helpful Tips:

- He should hold on to your hips with his hands as he strokes in and out.
- Tell your man to start slow and gradually pick up speed.
- Be sure to lean down on your elbows, not your hands for the most pleasure.
- Your man can use one leg to help him balance himself if he needs to.

## *Fun Fact*

*Most women will* **"queef"** *after this position. This is simply a "vaginal fart" and there is nothing wrong with it! This is common after vigorous sex that has pushed air into the vagina. It may be a little loud but it won't smell, and you and your man will get a good laugh out of it.*

# 6. THE FANTASY IN THE HAT

It can be hard getting men to open up about sex. Try playing a game to find out what he really likes.

Have him write down his top five fantasies and put them in a hat. Let him choose one fantasy out of the hat and fulfill it for him.  You should also try putting a few of your own fantasies inside the hat.

Make sure you act out his fantasy from start to finish and it will blow his mind!

# 7. TURN ON YOUR SEXY WHILE ON TOP

Men love watching their women on top. As you straddle his penis touch yourself slowly. Massage your breast while looking him in the eyes. Whisper something sexy like "I've missed feeling you inside of me". Tell him how good he feels inside of you. Give him a show he won't forget.

---

### Helpful Tip:

Use your hands. Place them on his chest, knees or even his arms or head and massage his as you move in a steady motion. Enjoy the ride lean back and let him watch you perform!

---

# 8. LOOK THE PART

Okay Ladies, this is a big one so pay attention! You've been working all day, cooking, cleaning, and the last thing on your mind is being sexy right? Well too damn bad! I know what you're thinking; "Damn DeShai. I thought you were on my side!" I'm on your side and that's why I'm telling you that you have to make time to be the sexy vixen he fell in love with.

Pull out some sexy lingerie and give him a treat. Always remember men are visual creatures, so looking the part is certainly a key factor in keeping your love life spicy.

# 9. DANCE FOR YOUR MAN

You don't have to be an expert to give a sexy dance. Put on some of your favorite music and perform for him. Don't be afraid to touch yourself and engage him. Remember to be confident.

# 10. LET HIM PLAY

Listen girl! It is okay for him to touch himself, so don't give him a hard time about it. When your man masturbates, it doesn't mean you're doing anything wrong or that he doesn't want you. Men love sex and trust me if you had to give it to him every time he wanted it then, you wouldn't be able to keep up!

Make it fun offer to let him watch you if he allows you to watch him. This makes for great foreplay.

# 11. LET HIM PULL YOUR HAIR

Get a little rough and let him pull your hair a bit. Now I know most "Sista Girls" like myself don't play about a good hair weave, but it's okay to switch it up a bit. Just make sure your hair is in there good girl!

# 12. GIVE HIM YOUR UNDIVIDED ATTENTION

Pay attention to him! This sounds so simple, but it can be a hard task. I find that sometimes in building a brand, raising a family, and trying to be superwoman; I neglect to pay attention to my king. Allow me to share something with you; inside of every man is a little boy who needs and wants your attention. That may sound a little weird, and I am in no way telling you to be a man's mother. I'm simply saying although men are tough on the outside, they want to know that you care about what they have to say.

# 13. HAVE SEX IN FRONT OF A MIRROR

You are beautiful! Your man loves you with every curve and roll. Trust me when I say he isn't concerned with your small cosmetic imperfections. Make love to him in the mirror, it will be fun! He'll love watch the two of you perform together.

# 14. COOK FOR HIM

It's not ALL about the sex, and sometimes, he just wants to know you care. Cook him his favorite meal and do it in something sexy. He'll love it, and if it's not tasty don't worry; all he'll be worried about is getting you out of that lingerie!

# 15. WAKE HIM UP WITH ORAL SEX

Men have always and will always love receiving oral sex. Take it to the next level by waking him up with some great oral sex.

---

Helpful Tips:

If you'd like to take oral sex with your man to the next level follow these useful tips.

- Keep it really wet always remember the wetter the better.
- Use your hands. Don't be afraid to use your hands for assistance and keep a nice grip on his penis.

Now we've talked about keeping it wet, but let's take it to another level! While giving your man oral, allow your saliva to drip down his penis. It will drive him wild.

---

### *Fun Fact*

*You may have been told that oral sex is safer than vaginal sex but that isn't true! Sexual transmitted diseases can be passed through oral sex also, so remember to always be safe and get tested.*

# 16. DON'T NEGLECT THE BALLS

The next time you're giving him oral sex, make sure you remember his balls. Sometimes women neglect them when giving oral because they have no idea what to do with them. If you want to make him weak in the knees include his balls in the festivities next time!

---

### Helpful Tips: Do's and Don'ts

### Do's:

- Suck gently on his balls when giving oral and caress his shaft.
- Rotate your tongue on his scrotum and lick his balls with long, sexy, gentle stokes.
- If you really want to blow his mind, flick your tongue rapidly but gently on his balls.

### Don'ts:

- Don't grab. The balls are a very sensitive area.
- Don't use your teeth, it could be painful.
- Don't squeeze, they aren't real balls!

---

# 17. KEEP YOUR HEELS ON

Take the sexy vixen role to the next level and keep your heels on. The visual of making love to you with your heels on will drive him crazy!

# 18. CARESS HIS FEET WHILE DOING REVERSE COWGIRL

This position should certainly be in your rotation. It's fun and a great way to switch up "riding". I've told you men are visual creatures so looking at you back side while you ride is always a plus for your man.

For the reverse cowgirl position you should be on top with your back facing your man. See the picture below:

---

### Helpful Tips:

- Maintain your balance by placing your hands on your man's legs or even gripping his ankles.
- Use your hands to help you move up and down on your man's penis.
- Try grinding on his penis and play with his testicles while you're moving.

# 19. LET YOUR CONFIDENCE SHOW

   Men love a woman with confidence and find it sexy. You don't have to be rude or cocky, but showing him a little confidence in bed will definitely turn him on.

# 20. ON BENDED KNEES

Variety is very important when it comes to keeping it spicy in the bedroom. I like to say that making the bedroom go boom should always be the goal. It can get a bit boring doing the same old positions too often.

Let's add a new one to the rotation: Sit in a lower leveled chair with your legs spread apart. Have your man bend down on his knees between your legs, lean back as he enters you and enjoy him.

# 21. ANAL

Okay, okay. You're thinking, "DeShai has lost her damn mind!" Don't skip this one!

Most women are afraid of anal sex for one of two reasons: they've heard horror stories about it or they've tried it and it was painful. If you've tried anal and it was painful, you were not doing it correctly.

Anal sex is pleasing to many men and women. There is nothing wrong with trying it with your man.

---

### Helpful Tips:

Take baby steps. Most couples make the mistake of trying anal sex from the back the first time. You should try the spooning position first, it's more pleasurable.

Take a warm bath before trying anal sex; remember to lube and to relax. Your man should never try to insert his full penis at once; you won't be able to take all of that no matter the size. Always remember that anal sex shouldn't hurt. If it starts to hurt you are doing something wrong.

---

# 22. LET HIM SPANK YOU

Tell your man you've been a bad girl and he needs to make you pay. Allow him to dominate you and give you a sexy spanking that you both will enjoy. He can use his hands or a whip, the choice is yours!

Don't be afraid to get into it and play the role. He'll like being in control, trust me.

# 23. GET NAKED

Have you ever kept your shirt on? Or even your bra because you're a little shy? You may even be self-conscious about your body. Girl take it all off for him and let your guard down. Let him feel your body against his body. You are most sexy in just skin!

# 24. KISS HIM DOWN THERE

When I speak to women, I often remind them that it's okay to be downright nasty with their men. Your bedroom is a place for you and your man to explore each other in any way you want.

Take "kissing his butt" to the next level. A man's anus is one of the most sensitive parts of his body and it's okay to explore that. The next time you're down there, try kissing or even licking, his butt.

---

### Helpful Tips:

- Use your tongue: place it flat and lick slowly then pick up speed. Make sure you flick it also.
- Kiss is anus while massaging his butt with your hands.
- Breathe softly against your man's anus as you moan.
- Remember to have your man clean and shave that area thoroughly.

---

### *Fun Fact*

*It doesn't mean your man is gay if he enjoys having his anus licked by you. There are tiny nerves in his anus that send pleasure to his penis when you lick it. Don't be afraid to discuss this with your man and remember to have an open mind.*

# 25. GIVE HIM A MASSAGE

Passion is a must in any romantic relationship. You have to keep the passion between you and your man going. Sometimes, we can find ourselves just going through the motions and having plain old sex. That's never a good thing.

Take some time out and give him a sensual massage. Rub him down while you tell him how amazing he is then make love to him right after.

Helpful Tips:
1. Light a few candles
2. Use fragrance oils
3. Use your thumbs on the insides of his shoulder blades and work them in a small circular motion. At the same time, use your other fingers to apply light pressure to the tops of the shoulder blades.

# 26. COPYCATS

Make it a movie night! Pop in one of his favorite erotic films and watch it with him. Try some of the moves from the movie and remember to have fun with it. He won't care that you aren't the world's greatest porn star because he'll be too happy you aren't turning your nose up at him for watching it.

I have listed a list of great exotic adult films for couples:

1. Shared Wives (New Sensations Studios)
2. Torn (New Sensations Studios)
3. Legal Appeal (Wicked Pictures)
4. Compulsion (Wicked Pictures)
5. Dinner Party 3(Adam and Eve Studios)
6. Dymes 4 (Afro-Centric Productions)
7. Chocolate Vanilla Cream Pie (Afro-Centric Productions)

---

### Helpful Tips:

- Watch the entire video before making love.
- Engage each other while watching by cuddling, kissing and teasing.
- Try giving him oral sex while he watches the video

---

# 27. GET WET

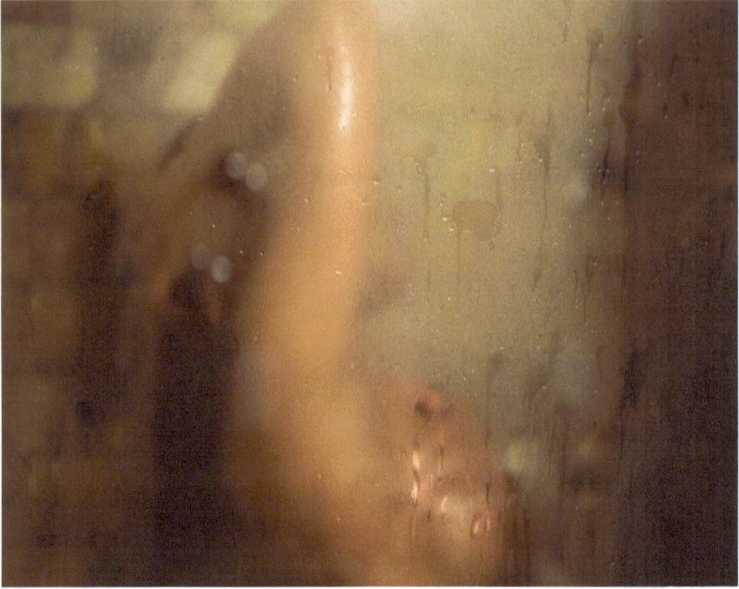

Don't be afraid to get your hair wet ladies! Jump in the shower with him or even try making love in the rain

Rubbing your wet bodies together will make the sex more sensual and passionate.

## 28. MOAN IN HIS EAR WHILE ON TOP

He'll love it when you're making sexy sounds in his hear. Take deep breaths and release them slowly and sensually in his ear. Nibble on his ear a bit while you moan.

## 29. DRIVE HIM CRAZY
### (In the car)

You don't always have to make love in your bedroom. Try being adventurous and get frisky in the car. When he's driving one day tell him to pull over and give him oral sex he won't forget. Climb in the seat like teenagers and have sweaty sex.

---

### Helpful Tips:

- The best time to try this is at night.
- Don't try this while the car is moving because it isn't safe.
- Try this in a low traffic area.
- You may want to crack the windows a bit
- Don't get too loud, you don't want to draw attention.

# 30. SEXY PHOTO SHOOT

Do something out of the box for him this year. Book yourself a professional photo shoot and gift him the pictures. He'll love looking at you and a sexy picture of you is better than a tie any day!

# EXTRAS

*Sexy Game Ideas It is important to keep your love life fun and spontaneous. You never want things to get boring between you and your man. Sometimes couples find that after being together a long time, things get a little repetitive or even predictable and you don't want that. Playing games makes for great foreplay and can keep you and your man both on your toes!*

*Check out some of the sexy games I love to play below:*

### The Panty Finder
Hide a few pairs of your sexy panties around the house for your man to find. Tell him that when he finds a pair of your panties, you will model them for him right on the spot.

### Role Play
This is an "oldie" but it's a lot of fun and certainly gets the job done. Act out your favorite movie or play a good old game of cops and robbers.

### Bed Bingo
Play a sexy game of bingo and the loser has to be the "Love Slave" for the night!

### Flirty Flash Cards
Create flash cards with sexy positions, acts and phrases and act them out with your man.

## Night Eye Spy

Put some of your favorite toys around your bedroom and have your man find them. Once he finds them, let him use them on you.

## Ice Pop

Grab some ice cream and have your man get naked. Put a spoon of ice cream in your mouth and then place his penis in next. The cold mixing with his warm skin will blow his mind!

*Your Notes & Personal Ideas* Use the next few pages to take personal notes and write down some of your own ideas for spicing up things. Think of some fun things you can do with your man and write them down so you don't forget them. Make a list of some fun games you can play together and come back to them later.

_____

_____

_____

_____

_____

_____

_____

_____

_____

_____

_____

_____

_____

***The Other 70 Percent*** *Without debate great sex should be at the top of your list when it comes to making the bedroom go BOOM; but believe it or not, it's going to take more than just sex to please your man. Early in this book, I told you that a couple spends more than seventy percent of their time outside of the bedroom. That means you have to have more than good sex to make a relationship work.*

*Sometimes understanding men can be like learning a new language and it just seems like they are just too damn difficult. I promise there are times I want to sell my hubby to the highest bidder, and then there are those days where no amount money in the world could make me give him up. I love him everyday and he makes me happy everyday. Now I didn't say ALL day every day, but he makes me happy all the same. You see that's how it is in relationships. You may often feel like you're in a game of "Love and War". The important thing to understand is that all days will not be sunny days and relationships are hard. When you care about someone, you do your best to understand him or her. We have to work to understand our men and how they communicate. Once you do that, dealing with them isn't so hard!*

*This section will consist of tips and insight on how you can better understand your man. Take it all in and the next time he makes you want to scream, use some of your newfound knowledge. It will shock him.*

# The No-No Chart

I like to call the chart below the "No-No" chart because it consists of things that can be the downfall of your relationship and send your man running for the nearest EXIT.

| | |
|---|---|
| Disrespect | In most cases, a man would rather go unloved than to be disrespected. Respect is important to him; you have to be tactful in the way you talk to him. |
| Mrs. Man | Your man doesn't want to be in a relationship with another man! Let him be a man. There is nothing wrong with being soft. |
| Nagging | Shut Up!!! Yep, you read right. Sometimes the best thing you can do is remain silent. |
| "Needy Needy" | Give him his space. Give him time to miss you. It's okay to be apart, you don't have to be joined to his hip all the time honey! |
| Jealousy | Don't be that girl! You know the one that is jealous of everyone. The one who can't stand for her man to even speak to anyone else. |

These are some of the things men "hate" about us and rightfully so. If you find yourself doing things on the No-No chart, check yourself and get it together!

Now let's cover some "must have" traits in pleasing your man. The chart below covers a few things a man looks for in a woman.

| | |
|---|---|
| Loyalty | Loyalty is a big deal to men. Your man wants to know that you have his back and will be in his corner when he needs you. |
| "Mrs. Cheerleader" | You should be your man's biggest supporter. He needs to know you believe in him and he wants to know you're rooting for him. Maybe he's applying for a new job or working on a new project; whatever it is, let him know you want him to be successful. |
| "Friends Forever" | He wants to be your friend. There is nothing more appealing to a man than the woman that knows how to be his friend first. He has to be able to talk to you without you going off the deep end or judging him. |

If you've got these main traits you're off to a great start!

We've covered the dos and the don'ts, and now it's time to talk about what he wants to hear. There are some things that you can say to your man that will make him happy and put a smile on his face. Take a look at some of the things you can say to your man to brighten his day below:

- **"I need you."** A man wants and needs to feel needed by the woman in his life. Hearing you say it will make his day. Take some time and just let him know that even though you're superwoman, you still need him!

- **"You look so damn good."** Yep, men want to know you think they look good. Let him know how amazing he looks to you, it will make him smile.

- **"Baby I love it when..."** Let him know when he does something you like! When he does something wrong you tell him, so let him know when he gets it right. He wants to feel appreciated too.

- **"You're right."** Now this one is going to be hard! If you're anything like me, you're never wrong. Admit when you're wrong and tell him not to get used to it!!!

- **"It's all about you today."** It's normally a man's job to do all the treating. Set a day aside to treat him to a sports event or one of his favorite activities.

# CONCLUSION

There is no argument that you and your man will clash, and this book is not the "end all be all," but it will certainly help you. You have to remember that anything worth having is going to take work. We have to make pleasing and appreciating our men priority. Try new things; research and take your relationship to the next level.

You should always be willing to explore and discover with your man. Remember that if you plan to spend a lifetime with this man, it's going to be a long ride, and you want it to be a fun, sensual, sexy and passionate one. Often women forget that men have needs just like we do. You've got a good, hardworking, wonderful man; he deserves to be catered to.

I hope that you will take the things you've read and apply them to your relationships. We all know my mission is to make bedrooms go BOOM one couple at a time.

Thank you for taking the time to read this guide, I am most grateful.

You may have questions or comments for me and I would love to hear them! Please send any questions or comments to **grownwomantalkent@gmail.com** and I will personally respond. We may even highlight it on the show or put it on the website!

www.ingramcontent.com/pod-product-compliance
Lightning Source LLC
Chambersburg PA
CBHW041800040426
42447CB00005B/275